Blues Legacy

Blues Legacy
Jacquese Armstrong

BROADSIDE LOTUS PRESS
Detroit

Copyright © 2019 Jacquese Armstrong

All rights reserved. No part of this book may be reproduced, stored in a retrieval system, or transmitted in any form by any means, electronic, mechanical, photocopying, recording, or otherwise without prior written permission, except in the case of brief quotations embodied in critical articles or reviews. Queries should be addressed to Broadside Lotus Press, Post Office Box 02011, Detroit, MI 48202.

First Edition

Front Cover Design and Book Layout
by Leisia Duskin

NLM Award Series Editor: Gloria A. House

ISBN 978-0-940713-27-7

Broadside Lotus Press
Post Office Box 02011
Detroit, Michigan 48202
www.BroadsideLotusPress.org

ACKNOWLEDGEMENTS

Several of the poems in this collection have been published previously in the following journals and anthologies:

Blackberry: A Magazine

Black Magnolias Literary Magazine

Day-One-E-Mag

For Harriet

A Gathering of the Tribes

GFT Presents: One in Four

The Rising Phoenix Review

DEDICATION

For my parents, George and Al,
the living legacies

CONTENTS

invocation of the ancestors   3
woke up this morning in the middle of a poem   4
sister from another planet   10
i'm black and i ain't apologizin for it   11
i miss my folks   14
blues legacy (standin at the crossroads)   17
don't insult my ancestors   19
do you hear the drums?   22
blue rose with thorns   24
"carolina shout"   26
"carolina shout" ii   Ecclesiastes (the preacher)   28
"carolina shout" iii   30
"carolina shout" iv the band's men   32
"carolina shout" v the club's patrons   34
Dinah Washington in the evening (trouble in mind)   35
notes on Archie Shepp, Princeton University, 12/2/17   36
my groove my face (a mild depression)   38
when rhythm met blues   41
when he gets the blues   44
midnight blues and hot chocolate   46
a kidnap poem   48
all images lead to music   50
tears   51
natural – just like music (a Marvin Gaye inspired joint you gave me)   53
queen own your crown   55
why i listen (to music) and don't watch tv   57
bizarre   58
the illusion of walls   59
sojourner   61

thoughts on camera wrought in blood tears   63
universal salutation   64
at a middle school voting site (10/16/13)   66
bus ride   68
blue   70
s i m p l e   73
learnin from double dutch and the blues   74
out on a limb   76
personal dis-ease   78
stand   80
radical kindness (this is my home)   82
i can hear him praying   85
dancin in the Light of my soul – anyhow   88
in our natural state   90
set the captives free   91
the final chord: a calling to my sisters (to all)   94

Blues Legacy

invocation of the ancestors

all that i am
i thank my ancestors for
the ones i see today
the ones i saw yesterday
the ones i know
the ones i don't know

the ones who occupied another land
the ones who were shackled in the hold of a slave ship
the ones who were sold like mules
the ones who worked the fields in sweltering heat
the ones who whispered
in the wings of "the big house"
the ones who made it to freedom
before emancipation
the ones who struggled for freedom all their lives
the ones who thanked the Lord
for secret communications
the ones who died in the struggle
the ones who pointed out to others
the direction to go
the ones who passed the secrets down
the ones who dared to be
the women and men in town

i draw on their Power
their Strength
keeps me.

**woke up this morning in
the middle of a poem in
the middle of a cry for humanity**

i can't recall
a language i feel

i can't recall
a language
i feel

i can't recall a language
i feel is my own

and you came to me with reason
and sanity but i heard
your voice in a language
not my own

you spoke it so
i could hear
i could see and feel
(but the language
       antiseptic
   not my own)

i
approach
this conundrum with a
sound no whimper no
weep no timidity of voice
we cop sound

sound
fills empty spaces
in castigated
  partitioned
souls

sound fills empty spaces
fills empty spaces of things
we know we have forgotten
but never knew

you sell your sounds American
among voices of hate
contempt
they use your sounds for their gain
(i guess you got to eat)

i clutch my sounds dear
to my chest
let them
approach a voicing
(i guess i'm lonely)

lonely
lonely for hunger and Truth
(i guess i'm lonely)
lonely
from the injustice
that robbed my cry
    (or wouldn't hear it)

lonely
hear my cry

tried to break it down
for every you to dig
like i heard in the 60s -- 70s
but that language
that language
never graced my ears
and so i alone
wolf the cry

wolf
the cry
that slept on a back porch
waiting
for a summons

wolf
the cry
keeps my soul in a state
of readiness
    (language not my own)

wolf
the cry
approaching that
        blues sound that
       jazz sound that
     hip-hop and even that
gangster that insists on callin me a slave name
('cause i know he's in pain)

i'm not angry
anymore
i just approach a sound
i can hear sounds
i can see sounds
can speak sounds
feel them

i clutch them to my chest my brother
'cause the killing has to stop

i clutch them to my chest dear brother
'cause the selling has to stop

i clutch
'cause contempt
hatred
fear
have to stop

i clutch them to my chest dear sister
'cause the self-hatred has to stop

i clutch them to my chest my sister
mourning
has to stop

as we approach
sound…sound…sound
our only language
all we know

i clutch it to my chest
tryin to approach a sound
every u could dig
as she said in a 70s poem
approaching sound

the remnants of our collective languages
(we are the melting pot of Africa)
approaching that lost legacy sound
a sound
to imitate a language
we lost
we never knew we had

sun is shining
   the weather is sweet
   make me wanna move
   my dancing feet
     to the rescue
here i am.*

i
am the rainbow
i will see
after the cloudburst
after the hail
   the storms

after the cry

and here i go
gathering sounds
to approach a language
i never heard
unable to forget

sound
approaching language
sound approaching language
Universal sound approaching
Love

a cry for humanity

Love and only Love can
translate.

*Bob Marley, "Sun Is Shining"

sister from another planet

rarely gracing the earth
with her presence
her "innertude" gets
provoked
by no-show folk.

(made her spiritual route
in decades embracing true ness
with a natural incandescence
preserving sanity)

the fight is on her terms only.

walks the
sojourner
following intrinsic signals
Home.

Home
where freedom
washes over the soul
like a clear running stream
the sky cries uncomplicated tears
and the wind is a silk cloak
wrapping the bareness of skin.

the trees laugh
in sympathy.

i'm black and i ain't apologizin for it

i travel back to the moan
at my birth's inception
the moan formed rhythm
       unguided
    spread through white cotton thorns and hot baked
sun
sheltered a people
of no common language

before
the working of a spiritual
before
the blues birth
before
any synthetically sung syllable
the moan
was
the travail of a mother in a long
                    labored
              birth

so i come back
'cause i know
my language
my
utterings
are not my own
      (i hear
        prosthetic voices
        mimic
        the night
        intense
            and i speak)

that's why i come back
to the moan
to
break my silence
to
break my fall
to
break my anger
and shatter illusive glass

come back to the moan

to feel

the embrace
        (you say resentment)
to feel camaraderie
        (you say distrust)
to feel the joy that is mine alone
    the creative spark
        (you say anger)
to feel
the truth

i get a flow
    a rhythm
        and my ancestors dance
across my page

(why would i re-jail them?)

so i travel back
to the moan
the start of my time
to check my pulse
and give back
to Caesar what is his.

i miss my folks

(this is my introduction
this poem is *not*
very pc
so if you're squeamish
close your ears)

i am *not*
a vegetarian
i eat meat
i enjoy eating meat
i come from a long line
of carnivorous
souls
i remember the smell of homemade sausage
original Kyles's recipe
"Mackel
(she never said Michael)
go get me that
pig."

my brother
only six
obeyed with
no thought

i
never watched the process
only
enjoyed the aftermath
and the smells
the smell of
collard greens
(cooked with pork)
lima beans
(cooked with pork)
green beans
(cooked with pork)
and of course pork
(cooked with pork)

i'm being facetious
of course
we ate other things

but it's funny how
you remember smells
like the smell of the fireplace
after it's gone out
and the cold damp
Alabama air
only shielded by quilts
pieced together by the hands
that made the sausage
picked and shelled pecans
for an entire family
cleaned other people's houses

and
i
have this picture
of my granddaddy
on my dreamboard
sitting
on the porch of his farm
in the middle of nowhere
Alabama
in a sport jacket
and hat
what i call
country-cool
like a Delta bluesman
in between sets
days i won't see any more.

blues legacy (standin at the crossroads)
Clarksdale, MS 12/26/16

Robert Johnson turned
face to the wall
recorded music we're still playin
after
standin at the crossroads.
(legend says he sold his soul
to the devil)

don't know
what i expected to see
ridin through the Delta

remnants of extreme poverty
picturin
sharecroppers like Muddy Waters
singin that juke joint blues
for 50 cents.

i thank God
some escaped.

(no crystalline words
portray the isolation
some live along
the road)

the sound
that blues sound
born on a ship
incubated in slave cotton fields
come to life in the voices of plantation
sharecroppers who worked
from dusk to dawn
with a penny to show
and some steam to blow off naturally
delivered to us now as
a sophisticated blues groove
that takes us in
to Saturday nights.

and they own it as "American" music
let's not forget where it came from.

don't insult my ancestors
(inspired by David Hammons's mixed media *Chasin the Blue Train*)

had to endure
soul destroying castrations
of mind from alabaster devils
tried to rob me of my pride
just to get to the Music

had me barin black
skin covered in drippin red
sore
to the touch
in sun-draining sweat
repeatedly until endless bales
were gathered daily
just to get to the Music

red-bottomed babies takin
my precious cocoa ones'
sustenance
callin me mammy
had to grow them
like my own
just to get to the Music

used me like livestock
even rented out my body
to produce more of me
to be beasts of burden used in the fields
like mules
so we hummed to conjure up power
just to get to the Music

put those dirt
sweat
filth-
filled clothes in scalding water pot
with lye that burned the innocence
off my hands
made those clothes wrinkle free
with hot steel as they sat watching
fanning themselves
just to get to the Music

had to move tons of coal
dust
invading my once healthy lungs
even moved them into the fire
day after day shovel after shovel
in sweltering heat stealin my last
breaths away
just to get to the Music

i was farming rented land and
what i raised from the blood of my brow
they ate the apples
juice runnin down their faces
threw the cores at me
chargin me for my rights
just to get to the Music

so don't inject that
my music is just American
don't tell me
my music
be a bastard child of uncivilized
beatings of the heart
only tribal inherited creativity

the more i survived the
twists and turns
of my mind
created time
it took to heal
puss-filled wounds
that refused to scab
because Bible-spoutin devils picked at them
daily

Music
fills any canvas
but don't brush stroke mine just American
it found me on a ship that
cast my brothers' wilted bodies
into the sea
made me envy
let me breathe.

do you hear the drums?

trees talk

winds listen to the defiantly mellow haunt of Billie whistling southern trees.

talk roots
with blood
bombarded and
internalize pain
like martyrs
speak from
inner rings protected
only by bark.

(know intimate details like
the oldest of lovers)

record centuries' mass
delusional tribes'
sport in trunks
roots
nourish hurt.

(winds cry cubic tears in summer)

trees talk
when we don't
shout
verbal war
our breath
suctioned from lungs daily
we cannot
cry.

(some get weary)

have witnessed
crimes heinous
over
a lifetime traumatized
they see

they speak.

are survivors
when green full
in stark barren winter
naked
shed no Light
victims
of oppression.

(the trees have always been my sisters)

trees
become a
dying species
commiserating with
the living
encourage accurate
history.

they talk

listen.

they beat the drums

hear them.

blue rose with thorns

blues
      and resilience
brought me forth
among cotton pickers
juke joint regulars' mason jars
full of hooch
Saturday night brawls
and Sunday-best pressed
seeking redemption of the soul

among the yahsuhs
and nawsuhs
and "crazy niggers"
who dared to
color in between the lines

among hearts
broken and pasted together
with sweat
dirt tears
that transformed them whole
through a family Love

among the educated
and subdued into
senselessness
living in fear of shadow

among artists
who dared to voice
among artists
who dared to play
among artists
sewing intricate

blood-stained blossomed tapestry of life
                    and chemists
                baking cakes

among swinging tree
festival sites
of "pick-a-nigger" injustices
by hungry hordes of animated
circus clowns

(and we dare remember the names
lives
of strange fruit with bowed head
tears)

amidst the hurting
and the loving
and the leaving

amidst the birth and death
and diaper changing
taking in others' wash
to feed hungry mouths
and all the other
stuff
that makes a life

i came forth.

i am jazz.

"carolina shout"
(inspired by Romare Bearden's *Carolina Shout* **and** *The Blues***)**

some
sparkling chocolate diamond women
get on stage
belt out a song strong
like blowin a horn full of air
in a quiet room
have whispered voices
let men pull the strings
on their person
like a purse
'cause that's all they think
they have

wave that laced handkerchief in the air
wearing orchids on the side
lookin uptown Billie sophisticated
bend to pick up that change
thrown at them for a tip

"carolina shout"
looks at her band
an assortment of broken brown-hued crayons
but swoon
they can make you swoon
play a tune that bends you over backwards
makin your lover jealous
play a song that takes you to an outer dimension
a place where
misogyny
and prejudice
are immobile—like stagnant air --
and everybody treasures themselves the way they are
so
purple is the color of the day
and the blues
just wash away
like sins in the river
at baptism

when
carolina shouts.

"carolina shout" ii
Ecclesiastes (the preacher)
(inspired by Romare Bearden's *Carolina Shout*)

these waters
were waded in cold
kept bounties off our backs
we've come full circle today
they'll wash all sins away

as i dip you down
in the murky river
think of Christ
and the remission of sins
ask the Father to forgive you
so you can begin again

without Christ's pardon
you'll be a wet sinner
without his Love
you'll feel the devil's crusty inners

shout! shout!
Hallelujah! Hallelujah!
the torn are made whole
the dime turns to gold
gathering at the water
somehow made safe
in these years we
admit our trepidations
to God
let Him sway our fears

so gather at the river
children
bring your families 'round
sing your soul to Christ
we will
chant down this town.

"carolina shout" iii
(inspired by Romare Bearden's *Carolina Shout* and *The Blues*)

and carolina used to sing
the gospel
eyes cast down in
false messiahed reverence
huddled over
feeling secular fists
sparring with spirit
in the preacher's delivery
of the "Word"
intricate gems of
iconoclastic knowledge
and gut-busting laughter
lured her away — she is
kaleidoscope blue today.

she huddled over
modeled like clay
subserviently humbled
to exalted man (who was he?)

never forsake the preacher's view
march every step in tune with his
paying your dues to him only

she pondered
if Salvation was free
why pay dues?
'cause she had no valleyed inner Light

the preacher
drunk with the wine of self
earthly rewarded
just another
factory assembled
prayed up wanna be servant

why should she bow
before his pedestal
when
God filled her chalice
daily?

carolina driven to a place
where breakdown was
as close as her shadow

she ran like water colors
that had too much
water
so hard and fast
ran into a brick wall

that's when
the blues
walked in.

"carolina shout" iv
the band's men (inspired by Romare Bearden's *The Blues*)

they looked like
butter wouldn't melt on them
i mean cool
but intricately wired
each in his own
musical time zone
music their only religion
playing
the sacrament
black notes dancing
on white paper encased in bars
the bread

they drank
more than water changed wine
the Bible – life
this was their world
smile as they did
wild as hurricane wind
on a beach
somewhere.

they gathered when blue darkness fell
hid in the Light
the brightness burned their eyes
parting the drapes on their
blue morbid fate

in truth
the clannish "Christians"
wanted them
too damned free
escaping the angular blind poverty
soul-sinking oppression
escaping the caged feel of "nigger"
on the skin
always on the run
in the know

they picked up their horns
preparing for sacrament
and began again
nightly.

"carolina shout" v
the club's patrons
(inspired by Romare Bearden's *The Blues*)

they show their white
        teeth
      prolonged
    loved to smile
the music's mood blue kaleidoscope
all night
no one gets bored
everybody with their uptown
        Saturday nite
      picture
    show
in real time
warmin the outside
inside
the libations
that constitute life.

Dinah Washington in the evening (trouble in mind)

articulate the blues
girl
'cause the sound
can drown
or make you laugh
(you choose)

but then you knew that.

notes on Archie Shepp, Princeton University, *12/2/17*

sadness is virtue is Light.
those fingers slender
white nails
never forgot a note
played
remember time
unproductive rhyme.

his breath
supplies fingers
and mind
their desire.

been blowin steam impressions
straightenin out lies on
fabric called America
blowin steam.

elegant cocoa fingers
take breath
regurgitate anger
through sound
'cause words ain't approachin feelin
(we know they say
we ain't "ish"
but what do we say?)

reality
dream pieces
construct sound
a durable fabric
a life
without distortion.

a time to live.
a time to relive.
no time to die.

ancestors encourage
blow your bitter-sweet poetic wind
till the last breath.

my groove my face
(a mild depression)

i groove
'cause my disinterest
takes me
where i want to go

i groove
'cause a band
entices my head
for days on end
i
am

fascination is a
coward
dis
taste takes on
a groove

i groove on Delta blues
and understand
meltin on a bleeding
syncopation that spills
guts
most convincingly
with a cool madness

i groove
regarding a jazz that
consumes the soul
yet rebirths it
    and blues
        and rhyme
so succinct
yet free
it makes a groove

Hendrix purple
on a mountain
cutting clouds from
a stance on
the watchtower
slicin air with fueled rhythm
he sets me out
and i groove
and the "girls"
enticin me to weep
'cause when the ladies speak
in a jazz tongue
i
flow
through the day
don't care
but hear
revere
talkin Carmen McRae
Cassandra Wilson
Billie Holiday
Abbey Lincoln
the sultry articulate flip of Dinah Washington
and did i say
Cassandra Wilson?

we birth
a spiritual
from blues so deep
the Universe opens
and accepts the notes

on this exhibit
i
stand

it gets me through the red days
what can i say?

when rhythm met blues

she told the seamstress
"put some rhysm in my dress
i want it to say my name
when i walk"

(the seamstress looked sideways
pursed her lips
but tried to fill her order—
how could a person not be able
to pronounce her own name?)

rhythm walked out
head in sky blue
wringin sway
African drumbeats ragin in her gait
her dress obedient
to her motion-filled mindset

on a side street corner stood
blues
broken down from years of
tawdry drinkin-till-dawn sets
but a smile wide white
against sepia smooth skin
shoes
mirrored wingtips
mocha and white
clothed for suiting
(not a wrinkle)

rhythm saw him
from a distance
curiosity always got her
in
trouble
but
what the hell

blues had his ancient eye
on that rhythmic sway the
dress was screamin
and he wanted to shout
no time for waiting
but made a most respectable approach

"shouldn't be out here alone miss"
he mused.

 "it is miss
isn't it?"

rhythm opened her mouth
but no words fell out
she hadn't stopped swayin
she never missed a beat

her non-stop music held him captive
in a jail of celebratory sound
fresh
not down home blue
he picked up on a natural
tune
and followed her in vocal ecstasy
"can i walk awhile?"
he said.

(blue cantankerous old mule
spies
young finger-poppin foot-stompin rhythm
and starts to plow
a new field)

when he gets the blues

when he gets the blues
the horn hollers soft
                sings brash
low down hustlin like
streetwalkers on a Friday night

i hear squalor
i hear rumor-filled middle-of-the-night laughter
undigested solitude
i hear my grandfather's one-eyebrow-raised
last instructions
i hear me
my mind being bruised
        and dizzied
    ripped and
torn
but then reborn
when he gets the blues

it's the only inspiration
to seed black fertile soil
in a space he doesn't own
when he gets the blues

old man walkin down the street
told me
daughter don't you worry
'bout the times
folks will lose their cash-molested minds
but you
got the blues behind
it's your inheritance
what you own

so
when he gets the blues
i sing
knowin
our souls are down-spiraling
into a blue
 echoed
  embrace.

midnight blues and hot chocolate

you don't want to get it
too hot
you'll never taste
the flavor
not too cool
'cause you'll drink it down
too fast
you don't want to be too thirsty
you want to savor
the flavor
like the blues at midnight
you want to set it out
just right

midnight blue
sharin with the stars
a little gin and rye
hot chocolate blending
elemental
sweetness and comfort
depth of flavor
the moon invades

midnight blue
takes over senses
not lonely
but sullen
contemplating
wondering
ready to glide
at a moment's notice

hot chocolate warm
brown
welcoming
you embrace the cup
like home embraces
you.

a kidnap poem

why have you
kidnapped my poems
and held them hostage?

you run round and round
my head
tying it up
with silly notions and carpets
on air

i need to work.

why
has your smile so
captivated my thoughts that
it is as constant as the illuminated moon?

i have lots to do.

why is it that i
can hear your voice
calling my name in that
                    slow
                sweet
            textured
         honey
southern drawl
gently rocking like a
horse-drawn carriage in Central Park?

there i go again.

why can't i just admit that i
am insane and
want you to be insane with
me?

wonder why?

all images lead to music

loving is
like the perfect scent
of jasmine on a summer-felt day—
the mellow mind sound of Isleys in the mist
the incessant winter white petals
of Japanese cherry blossoms
falling to the ground
like snow—
the echoing sound of Phoebe
like a cool clear running stream
the sunrise
with my hazy shade of purple giving texture
like a raspy Billie tune
the sweet bitter of dark chocolate
the quenching taste of water
after many hours of thirst—
familiar
like an old Al Jarreau song
it's a want
          that you think you need
like shelter
until you're homeless
like clothes
until you have only those on your back—
you feel your insides touching and
much regal roughness and nonchalant texture
irreverent
like classic Joan Armatrading
but the want
beautiful
like Grover
anytime
nice mellow bloom.

tears

intimate public
display in glass case
cracked
streaming down
making ridges in brown skin
parted like banks
of one river's undetermined path
necessary to relieve pressure
on too full cookers
ready to blow.

(have been blood
        square
    crystals
held back with a dam of indifference)

they talk
never audibly
let cry have his way
muffled but screaming
a kick in the gut
can make teeth wrench.
the mouth
wide open.

tears have been mist
from
temporary insanity's
play
an occasional weighted
drop
like a block of concrete
into water.

you have to earn
their retreat
when pain set aside
takes on vivid
hues.

Natural -- just like music (a Marvin Gaye-inspired joint you gave me)

slide earphones on
layer the music
over noisy abstractions
coat my mind in your soul's
music—

                                       makin it a solid
                                                 blue
                                                 funky
                                               mellow
                                         groove that
                                          could last

your smile
sings intense
cause i don't hear
words
(just like music)

what did you say?
my mind skipped
a beat
and i'm trippin
on an island
of everafterness
(just like music)

but i'm
gonna make this simple
you
kinda make my eyes dance and
i'm on an endless river bank
fuchsia rose petals under feet
forgetting smog
political
ramifications personal philosophies
existential wastelands dreamin up
theories for irrational letters
and rust
        it's just like music

mellowed stars twinkle twinkle
restin in my eyes
i'm goin in for the layered
abstracted
melt of a "flo"
        just like music.

rhythm of a falling star
ignites passion
like a flowering hyacinth bed
my eyes veiled
takin over spirit
music—
i feel your soul.

queen own your crown

don't you let that tear
rob you
of your majesty
don't let anything rob you
of your Joy
not that
solitary moment
that tries to introduce
doubt
not that glimpse of darkness
that tries to drive away
the Light

the solitary tree
naked will soon
be cloaked in green

and when the wind blows
harsh
remember
it can
caress

and when the Sun
beats down at times
know you can't exist
without its Light

and if your dress is shabby
your shoes less than new
and you're battle-weary
and it obscures your view
cry a little smile
bathe in the Master's Love

your magnificence
even in this time
you can carry

own your crown queen
own your crown

though it be invisible
own your crown.

why i listen (to music) and don't watch tv

the money soldiers line up
like the million Grace Jones
dolls in demolition to pry your soul
loose from its integrity

they sell cheap dreams

tv invades a
once-innocent brain
and takes human dignity
infusing limitations
to line unrestricted pockets

castigates imagination
for being
the technicolor response
in the brain's capacity
to absorb
anything

Music
is vibe Eternal
and
i dig it.

bizarre

ever have a day
when
all thoughts collide
bouncing off skull
sides
settling
to blow your mind
like popcorn
on hot grease

makes ya eyes lock in ya head

(a day like any
other day
until…)

bizarre second comings
and goings
and
    yes
this leaves the mind blank

the plants still shine green
the sky still cries hazy blue
color courts a montage of flowers
but a difference
a veil covers the mind
and eyes prop open
daylight is of no significance
and every word
has a different meaning.

i mean
       totally bizarre.

the illusion of walls

Faith (the substance of things Hoped for)
should flow like a river
anticipating a breeze

(should be non-exclusive
meditating on the present
birthing a Future not frigid
from the cold air of entitlement)

there are no compartments
to inhabit as mongrels
comb occupied territory

(we are
consciousness
bathed in Grace
together
we are God
control the Universe)

my ancestors died in Hope
now i
am imprisoned by it
we stand from birth

trees understand
they grow
together
or apart
do not shun different species
in their air space

we need them to survive.
(fear is the wall that permeates consciousness
with hate)

pay attention
to detail.

    the Universe is listening.

sojourner

she carries her Africanness upright
as an indomitable princess warrior
able to do battle with demons and
enemies of Time.

He set me over my inheritance
ground my ancestors trod
since time started
i
a mighty African princess warrior
set with Sword
and Staff
He let me roam the jungle
at will
      (He only gives you as much
       as you can bear)

the jungle is mine
the stalking lion knows my name
and handles me
as one of his own
my place at the watering hole
is prime

  (she carries her Africanness
  the badge of strength
  promise
  she is always the warrior)

i must cover the earth on foot
never knowing what will come
before me—i only envy the birds

He set me with an endless cup of spirit
to do battle with those
who would try to invade my post
(they think me vulnerable)
i like to play with them
watching them fall into my traps

  (she carries her Africanness
  wise
  disguising the third eye)

i will battle indelibly over my inheritance
the sacred ground i was taught
to treasure
and keep
through any storm or gale
it is the gift of God and the ancestors
not to be squandered
to keep precious
i am protective of my ancestors
and their gifts

i am the warrior
but i laugh often
ancestral ground is everything

she
carries her Africanness
upright with promise
wise
she
is a warrior
you will never truly
know her.

the mind is her inheritance.

thoughts on camera wrought in blood tears
"Those who commit the murders write the reports."
Ida B. Wells (1862-1931)

you
hear no voices in color
dub them
cartoon characters unreal
(perhaps you think they will
rise again after you shoot
displaying a hole that will disappear
in the next frame)

cynicism is your religion

your bosses paint dynasties
and invoke consumerism
on color-created flow
make attempts
at using crayons
inside lines of wrath
(color is brilliant

survives)

the system is your super hero cape

your fatalistic systems
conjure
a turtle's pace genocide
of red-stained knives reflected
on color

you insult our worth.

universal salutation

heard an
Asian teenager
greet his Asian friend
"my niggah"
had to turn around to
discover the ethnicity

bastardization of a
bastard word? does
it make the unworthy hello
lukewarm for us? and
why did we start
using the hateful expression
as endearing anyway?
in spite?
to turn the universe inside
out?

does a teenager understand the history
of hate
mockery
contempt
that travels with the word?
do we?

all smiles in a greeting
the handshake pullin
you to my chest a
symbol that you are close
to my heart
my niggah

but man
when you say that
i know you don't see
our magnificence when
you look in
a mirror or in
my eye.

at a middle school voting site (10/16/13)

i saw you today
a little boy with
Coke bottle glasses
two steps out of line
but finding your way
if only to class

i saw you today
my little brother
in a clowning crowd of your peers
with a thought balloon
always above
that
never quite matched the environment
i saw you today
              a
            lone
           black
          seed
        in
a sea of white faces
and i thought…
i saw you today
    in a George
        Washington
          Carver
            Halloween
outfit provided by your scientist dad

passing out peanuts
and teaching
always teaching
that sea of white
we knew so much about
that never knew us
i saw you today my little brother
i saw me today my little mirror
i saw us
only survive because we dared
to put both fingers in the air
and walk away.

bus ride

he
got on in a force field of funk
Bose surround sound funk with
a residual factor
swag like he had taken a bath
one day

funk that
reaches up your nostrils and
makes ya eyes lock in ya head

this poem is dedicated
to him.

retroactive funk
kickin my butt
after a particular rider
gets off the bus
and before his friend gets on
the processional funk
hits the air

and then there's the
kind
that smacks u
in the face
and it's always champ

confrontational funk
no matter how you struggle
to get away from it the
smell follows you

so
i discretely smell my clothes
'cause this odor is so close
to home
i call it clandestine funk
it wants to make a rendezvous

and we can't forget
anonymous funk
u don't know where it's
comin from
but you smell it
and i know this isn't the
George Clinton definition
(especially since
this brand of funk is
equal opportunity)
but here i sit
classifyin funk
to take my mind off the stench
that isn't on a slave ship
(or is it?
whole "nother" poem)

but at the end of the ride
desegregation funk kicks in
you don't know where
one funk begins
and the other ends.

blue

and i am inside my mind
controlling the levers that
guide my lifeless shell
through the universe
the machine is outdated

every highway a
dead-end street
to insanity-in-a-box
lost in space like
Will Robinson

rising at noon i
pull the shades down
drown in mattress and
pillow again smother
my head in
cover i
am an ostrich
i don't want to know

three-fried brain
hollowed eyes sinking
like a raft with a hole
down
to my concrete feet

see black in
Light
grey storm skies
optimistically embraced like
a childhood buddy
lost to the rains
the air's stench can't upset me
corrugated skin and i
could care less about exfoliation
my mind left without me

wrap myself around myself
in a corner so tight i
can't rock
head on knees
no tears a
straitjacket looks
inviting
i am not lucid

winter sings arias January
through January in an irritating
mezzo-soprano the
bareness of trees in thick wind
like dinosaur bones in a small room exhibit
i am
frightening
smoking Newports 24/7
it
satisfies my taste for
food pacing the floor
guarding the door
from thought police 'cause
they may storm in
and arrest my carcass

*(and when someone makes
you laugh you
envision being with them
forever
no cost)*

guilty innocence
brown-grey the
stylist's dream thoughts
on a loudspeaker
like the cars rollin
through the streets
i think i'll go dig my grave

Stepford Wives's presentations
grey ghost gives
up the life

not looking back.

s i m p l e

comin to it
honestly
the blues that is

comin to it
correct
knowin i
can't go under
round the sides
or over
i must go through

comin to it
honestly
like Adam to God
after the fall in
the Garden
when the blues walked in

comin to it correctly
with the fervor of Nat Turner
on his mission
correctly
with all intellectual knowins and prowess
all feelins
like a bluesman
in between molten midnight sets
standin up straight and tall
like ya daddy taught ya

the blues look simple

till you start
playin 'em.

learnin from double dutch and the blues

never learned double dutch as a child
we only used one rope
but
the blues trained me
for double dutch
(that signifyin stylin smilin profilin kinda thang) u

know i been dodgin
bullets and thangs for years
(had to get my timin straight)
jumpin into action
i ain't spose to be in
duckin my head
at every turn
but i mostly
fell over myself doin it
dutch gave me a dose of
discipline

the blues said dodge
until you fall out
then you'll know
what you can take

so why kill the blues
it taught me
taught me well

and when
that blatant enigmatic racism
gets thrown
i laugh
send those bullets back
or dodge 'em
with the style and grace
only my momma coulda taught
long as they can throw 'em
i can junk 'em

i got the blues in me
done lasted 400 years
it can last 400 more.

out on a limb

i sit
overlooking city
mellow cobalt sky
marveling at the size of the moon
revisiting sins of
strata past
for this
i am called a martyr
or so the illusion passes

(i have moved to the
off center of the bough
one too many times
moved to a higher limb
before the cradle fell)

i am an artist.

my limb overlooks
the banks of a still
river
where you sit
contemplating?

i want to warn you.

silence
can be your enemy
share your thoughts
or kaleidoscope blue
engulfs you
mesmerizing at once
then imprisoning

step away.

thoughts
have been known
to be incendiary

i am not afraid.

tell me yours.

personal dis-ease

apathy the numbing disconnect crept in veins once active
    with red blood cells

(the vampires have done
their jobs)

(i look at a video in disbelief)

so what
was he thinking the second before he shot him --

"i'm gone kill me one today
just want to know what it feels like" ?

sounds like a line said out loud in one of those info movies
wrought of deep white southern violent
         oppressive indifference to
acknowledgement of civil rights

(there is a numbing disconnect from the Maker)
i had often asked myself   if i could have been at
Selma   or a lunch counter   or
any protest during   the Fight

could i have had the courage to practice non-violent civil disobedience?

'cause see here's the thing
i know my feces stink do those who
would ignore life's worth?

see i'm not really sure

'cause if they did wouldn't they see me?

(visiting a colonial home i listened to a tour guide
expound but the only fact i really heard
slaves also wiped their masters' behinds after they
voided)

i realize i live purely in theory won't participate in
anything i can't understand and yet even my theoretical
self knows

there is a connected Consciousness

if we all disconnect choose violence or apathy there will
be a shift more intolerant than
the time you're reading these words
the atmosphere jaded
becomes
the acid rain

and so personal dis-ease becomes the kaleidoscope
focus

(i practice radical kindness
my life and Spirit are as
important as yours)

i must answer to my Maker.

stand

i stand
because a multitude
of ex-slaves
nursed my wounds
bandaged my head
as i lay in
catatonic blue.

the mind is
a lonely and complex
environment.

voices will collide
and fight
for a morsel of dominance.

(they ignore you and
fight each other over
your mind.)

laugh at the private hellhole
and the public circus comes
blazing.

born to be a survivor
dating back
to a ship
where you were told
to forget your name.

(see
we've got this fortress
of hope built around us
doors chained
no matter what happens
we stand.)

radical kindness
(this is my home)

so i walked away
both fingers in the air
to save myself
early on
and fumed for decades

(the instigator never knew me)

had me singin blues
i can't even subscribe to
buryin my ashes in Niger
with no home
and a continent
that didn't know me

see
i missed the point

(no time for victimization)

i missed
the
    point.

blood pourin in the streets
they call it rain
and when we leave red footprints
want us to clean the non-existent

this is my home.
(just thought i'd say that)

that being said
how can they disrespect me
in my own house?

(i have to allow it, don't i?)

i built this house more than
four score and seven years before
Lincoln opened his mouth

i'm no longer singin
songs of exclusion
        'cause this is my house

i shout i am
    because
i am
          this is my house

won't tolerate that psychological
defense mechanism apathy to
drown my voice

(and i caress the wings on my soul)

i have to continue
to care.

i have to continue to care.

i have to continue
to care
    and care for all
even the ones who perpetuate their fallacy of
superior distinction

i was made fit
for the Fight
and it's in me
to just be
and tell you

this is my home.

i can hear him praying
Colonel A. Thomas (1902-2003)

granddaddy wasn't long-winded
in daily conversations
but when he started to pray
you knew you were going to be
a while

"Oh God our help in ages past…"

the salutation was
the longest part
you just knew the Lord was
more than magnified and smiling
by the time he got to
the crux of the matter

"…our hope for years to come…"

next came the Lord's prayer
and the blessings he
asked for
blessings for everyone
on the planet namely
one by one

"…our shelter from the stormy blast…"

the crux of the matter may have been something
as everyday as
the blessing of the food

"…and our eternal home…"

when he prayed
you could almost see God
nodding and smiling saying
well done my servant Alfred

"Our Father which art in Heaven..."

now for the close
he always gave the same number of points for this
'cause he went over every accolade in the salutation
and asked God to continue to be that

"...hallowed be Thy Name..."

in his everyday conversation
granddaddy called Him the Master
and you knew
he could go to the door and knock
be let in
and have long philosophical conversations

"...Thy Kingdom come..."

in later years (after 100)
he would say
i didn't get a word
from the Master today
in reference to his departure from earth

"...Thy Will be done..."

this was a man who with his wife Lena
saw six children through college
in Jim Crow Alabama on
non-existent wages
and separate but equal formal education
his prayers protected
and made everyone
prosper

*"...and we will continue to give You the Praise
the Honor and the Glory..."*

granddaddy woke me up at midnight
to remind me of this

(i asked God for a thread and
He sent His servant Alfred with a rope)

"Amen."

8/17/13
dancing in the Light of my soul -- anyhow

the light plays
tricks
with an evolving
revolving
mind
shows sinister shadows
stops movement

but in the soul
the Light is pure
(when you ask)
it's like the Sun shining in the pouring rain
whose attention
commands yours -- He
is life

colors are music
never separate
and my feet command the distance
my soul at peace
i hug
the insides
never lie

there are no words
'cause in Light
they don't exist
sound motion articulate movement
circular
arms crossed
guarding chest
and tears
don't matter
sensitive smiles
tolerated

dancing in the Light
no guilt confesses pain
arms stretch wide
head arches to feel
White Light touch
from the Maker
of my soul.

in our natural state

i fell
asleep on the back of a swimming
green
sea turtle
huge by my standards
but he carried me far away
far away from my home

i was in a land where
no one
had wings
especially not colorful ones
they felt constrained by their very own
presence
i thought it strange
that these creatures with so many devices
would be so sad

at home
we don't own
we don't create
we don't think most of the time
we fly.

set the captives free

and they came in droves
to save my then
non-existent soul

they cared.

tell the story

a lady
with a jar of water
and some stale biscuits
packed them for me
she said the journey
would be long
gave me a handkerchief
old tattered worn

"you will cry"
she said.

gave me her bandana

"you won't have time
to fix your hair"

the last thing she gave me
the Bible she said she
couldn't read

"you can"
she said.

tell the story

man in overalls
whitest tee
shirt

"you will have to bend
your back" he said
"but don't let them break it."

tell the story

the children
scattered
scorned
driven before time

you got to play?

you'll see another day.

giving their best smiles
it was all they had.

and one by one
they laid gems at my feet
until i
in my innocence
overwhelmed them
burdened them
with my confusion

then
just knowing
silent closed-mouth smiles.

you will live to see
captives set free
your eye
will tell you different.

the final chord:
a calling to my sisters (to all)

my sister
you are significant
you are
the torchbearer
that keeps the world
from darkness

because it is the Light
in our souls
that keeps the world from
complete darkness
hold onto that Light
feed it oxygen
make the flame grow higher

because
we
write ourselves
into existence
and we
create the screenplays
that will play out
tomorrow
and the next day
and the next day

we have that power

and that power cultivates change
as sure as a certain seed cultivated
will grow blossoms

the negative forces
camp around us
they push they prod
cynicism is the child
of egocentricity and
negativity—
don't play with him

(hold on a change is coming)

i can't afford extravagance
i would rather see the Sun
(hold on we make the change)

we think
we say
we act
and in a synergistic way
that becomes reality

we write ourselves into existence

in a thousand tomorrows
and the next day
all orchestrated
by the soul full music
of pen strokes and imaginings
we
are significant
descendants of the Highest

evolution of the Universe
is in our hands
when we write ourselves into existence

my sister
you are significant
when you are positive
you are the torchbearer
that keeps the world
from darkness.

ABOUT THE AUTHOR

Jacquese Armstrong is a poet and writer residing in Central New Jersey. Her first poetry chapbook, *dance of the shadows*, was released in June 2017. She has been published in *For Harriet*, *A Gathering of the Tribes*, *The Rising Phoenix Review*, *Black Magnolias Literary Journal* and *Ourselves/Black*. Ms. Armstrong received the 2015 Ambassador Award of the State of New Jersey Governor's Council on Mental Health Stigma, for promoting wellness and recovery, and reducing stigma through the arts.

www.ingramcontent.com/pod-product-compliance
Lightning Source LLC
Chambersburg PA
CBHW071009160426
43193CB00012B/1977